COMFORT FOR
A WOMAN'S HEART
SUE REIDELL

Comfort for a Woman's Heart
by Sue Reidell
Copyright © 2018 Sue Reidell

ISBN 978-1-63360-102-4

For Worldwide Distribution   Printed in the U.S.A.

Urban Press
P.O. Box 8881
Pittsburgh, PA 15221-0881 USA
412.646.2780
www.urbanpress.us

FOREWORD

I had a lot of fun writing *Comfort for a Woman's Heart*. Any time I have a chance to share my favorite Scripture verses and pictures with you is a delightful blessing for my heart and soul.

God is my writing partner, and we wrote this book especially with you in mind. I hope and pray that you have many enjoyable moments as you digest each devotional and inspirational picture into the innermost parts of your being, and allow them to satisfy the craving of your soul with a comfort and peace that can only be found in the loving presence of God.

As you read, please keep in mind one of my favorite Scripture passages, which has been important to the healing of my own soul:

> Seeing then that we have a great High Priest who has passed through the heavens, Jesus the Son of God, let us hold fast our confession. For we do not have a High Priest who cannot sympathize with our weaknesses, but was in all points tempted as we are, yet without sin. Let us therefore come boldly to the throne of grace, that we may obtain mercy and find grace to help in time of need (Hebrews 4: 14-16 NKJV).

May God bless you through each devotional reading and picture.

Sue Reidell
Pittsburgh, PA
November 2018

DEVOTIONAL 1

"Whoever believes in me as the Scripture has said, 'Out of (her) heart will flow rivers of living water" (John 7:38 ESV).

May this breathtaking waterfall comfort your heart, no matter what is going on with your day. Imagine that the Lord created this waterfall just for you. It is an image to remind you that He delights in showering upon you healing waters to refresh your troubled soul with peace and serenity.

Dear Heavenly Father, I thank and praise You for always delighting in me. I am blessed to have a Father who is overjoyed to meet His daughter's every need! Amen

DEVOTIONAL 2

A person's steps are directed by the Lord. How then can anyone understand their own way? (Proverbs 20:24).

If you follow the perfect plan of the Lord's steps, it will resemble a mosaic and your life will go smoothly with joy filling your soul every second of your day. You will help others with whom you come in contact to praise the Lord as your light shines brightly from within.

Dear, Lord, I am blessed to have You guide my footsteps through life. I can't make it or live without You, precious Father. You are everything to me and I am thankful to be Your daughter.

DEVOTIONAL 3

Seeing then that we have a great High Priest who has passed through the heavens, Jesus the Son of God, let us hold fast our confession. For we do not have a High Priest who cannot sympathize with our weaknesses, but was in all points tempted as we are, yet without sin. Let us therefore come boldly to the throne of grace that we may obtain mercy and find grace to help in time of need (Hebrews 4:14-16).

Jesus is always present and available to comfort you. He will never turn you away, for our Lord loves His children very much. Seek His comforting sanctuary where Jesus holds you in His gentle arms until all the tension of your day just fades away, and joy takes its place in your soul.

Lord Jesus, You are my comfort in both good and bad times. I love how You wrap Your gentle arms around me. No one else can satisfy all my needs like You can. I love You, Jesus, so very much.

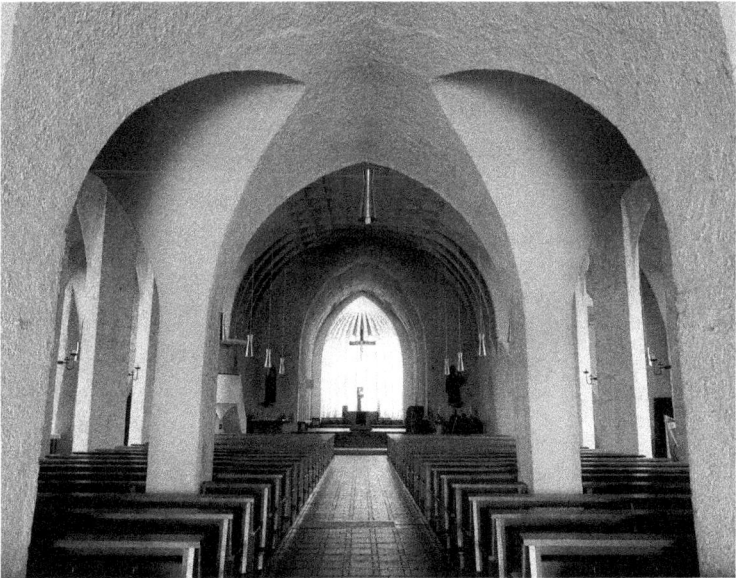

DEVOTIONAL 4

"So do not fear, for I am with you; do not be dismayed,
for I am your God. I will strengthen you and help you; I
will uphold you with my righteous right hand"
(Isaiah 41:10 NIV).

Praise God with uplifted hands to the heavens, singing and dancing as you glorify His Holy Name. He deserves your praise as you humble yourself on bended knees. God is good all the time, and all the time God is good!

Thank God for His mighty strength that defeated all the giants that have come to battle you. He struck each giant down with just the touch of His finger. Afterwards, God held you by your hand as together you walked over your fallen enemies, victorious with God at your side.

Oh, how I love Thee, God of my heart and soul. You never
let me down when I call on You for help. I am victorious
when I say the name of Jesus. How faithful You are, God,
to serve and uphold me with unconditional love. What a
precious Father God I always have by my side.

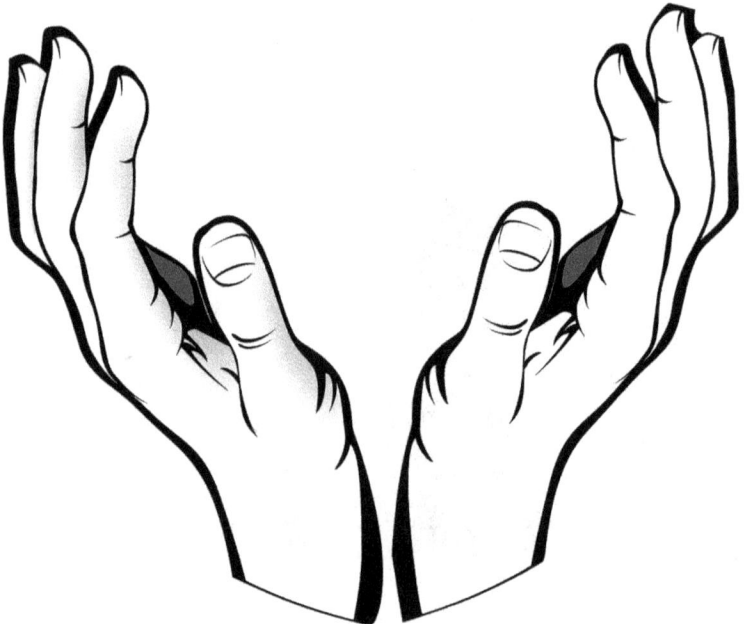

DEVOTIONAL 5

*The Lord is my shepherd; I shall not want. He makes
me to lie down in green pastures; He leads me beside
the still waters. He restores my soul; He leads me in the
paths of righteousness for His name's sake* (Psalm 23:1-3).

Picture yourself lying down on a meadow in the presence of
the Lord. Look out over the clear blue waters of a lake before you and
relax in the gentle, comforting arms of the Lord. Imagine all your
worries being tossed into and sinking to the bottom of the lake, never
to bother you again. When you trust in the Lord, blessings will show
up when you least expect them.

*Lord God, I am blessed to have a loving and
compassionate Companion like You in my life. When I
am troubled and worried, You run after me and sweep
me into Your comforting arms, and gently lie me down
in a beautiful meadow, overlooking a clear blue lake,
blessing me with Your peaceful presence.*

DEVOTIONAL 6

And give thanks for everything to God the Father in the name of our Lord Jesus Christ (Ephesians 5:20 NLT).

Your Best Friend picked this magnificent favorite-colored rose from His precious garden in heaven as a gift of love to you, to delight your soul with its healing fragrance of tranquility, peace, and bliss.

I want to shout from the rooftops how thankful I am for Your compassion and kindness, Lord. I could never have a better Father who is so thoughtful in surprising His daughter with the most extravagant gifts imaginable to enchant her heart and soul, accompanied by His priceless treasure of unconditional love. I am captivated with the rose You sent me from Your heart to mine!

DEVOTIONAL 7

Jesus Christ is the same yesterday, today, and forever
(Hebrews 13:8).

What is written in the Holy Scriptures is all true. Therefore, you can be assured that Jesus will never abandon you so you have to fend for yourself to battle this dark and evil world. His holy Word declares that Jesus will never leave you nor forsake you. He will be with you to the end of the ages. This is a solid promise you can place in your soul to secure great comfort and peace knowing you are never alone, because Jesus will always be beside you.

Jesus, You are a great and awesome Provider! I am grateful knowing You are my constant Companion through all the rest of my days on this earth. I find such comfort and peace reading the Holy Scriptures every day. I feel Your divine presence, Lord, with every word I read. I never want to be far from You. I love You, Jesus, so much!

DEVOTIONAL 8

*For while we were still weak, at the right time Christ
died for the ungodly. For one will scarcely die for a
righteous person—though perhaps for a good person
one would dare to die—but God shows his love for us in
that while we were still sinners, Christ died for us*
(Romans 5:6-8 ESV).

Just think of God like a delicious piece of chocolate that melts
in your mouth, comforting and satisfying you as you savor its flavor.
God knows all about you. You can't hide anything from God. He
always accepts you just the way you are. You never have to pretend
you are something you are not. What's more, God will never judge
you.

If God would send His Son Jesus to die in your place for sin-
ning against Him, then there is nothing God will not do for you. His
unfailing love for you is never-ending!

*Holy Father God, I can't fully understand how much
You love me, but I guess that is the point. I don't have
to understand Your thoughts. Your thoughts, God, are
higher than my thoughts, for they are perfect. I only have
to accept that Your unfailing love for me will never end.*

DEVOTIONAL 9

Fear of the Lord leads to life, bringing security and protection from harm (Proverbs 19:23 NLT).

The Lord is vigilant to ensure that His children are protected and come to no harm. His omnipresence permits Him to be present everywhere you go. He is your faithful bodyguard, and you never walk alone! Those the Lord loves, He shields with His presence 24 hours a day, seven days a week.

Gracious Heavenly Father, I am overjoyed to have You with me wherever I go. Nothing can harm me, Lord, with You as my bodyguard. Thank You, Father, for being so vigilant in watching over me.

DEVOTIONAL 10

For God gives wisdom and knowledge and joy to a
(woman) who is good in His sight (Ecclesiastes 2:26).

When you gaze at this awe-inspiring picture of the sun setting over the ocean, how can you not believe that God is infinite in His wisdom? Man didn't create the world in six days. God called the world into being to captivate the heart and soul of His children. He knew all the trials and tribulations you would face each day. Ultimately, God gave you a pleasurable trip away from all that disturbed you into His presence through His magnificent creation. Yours can be contentment and serenity in every enthralling glance at the spectacular scenery He created that surrounds you.

What can I say to all the blessings You, my Lord, have
given me to enjoy to my hearts contend? I know I don't
deserve such generosity from You, Father, because of
all the times I disobeyed Your will and went my own
way. But, gracious Father, You delight in seeing me
happy. Thank You, thank You, thank You, God for Your
compassion and kindness towards me. I love You with all
my heart and soul!

DEVOTION 11

Do not let your adornment be merely outward—
arranging the hair, wearing gold, or putting on fine
apparel—rather let it be the hidden person of the heart,
with the incorruptible beauty of a gentle and quiet spirit,
which is very precious in the sight of God (1 Peter 3:3-4).

Be like a newborn baby, adorable and sweet, needing the gentle touch of its mother to comfort it. A baby lies secure in its mother's womb for nine months, then comes out subject to the evil of this world. It can't take care of itself and needs constant care from its mother.

Just like a newborn baby, you need constant care from God. No matter how many times you dress up the outside of your body, it's the inside of your soul that needs to be dressed up and taken care of by God. The reality is that your body will someday die. You have a choice, however, so your soul can live forever with God. Only God can repair the damage you did to your soul by allowing sin to rot it away, but only if you ask Him to do so.

Dear Precious Healer, I need Your gentle touch to
comfort the inner parts of my soul. I have for so long
dressed up the outside of myself, like a mask of deception.
Now I am asking You to please, Father God, dress up my
soul, making it new again as You clean all the filthy sin
out of it. I want to be a brand new creation in You, like a
newborn baby coming out of its mother's womb.

DEVOTION 12

O Lord, God of Israel, there is no God like you in all
of heaven above or on the earth below. You keep your
covenant and show unfailing love to all who walk before
you in wholehearted devotion (1 Kings 8:23 NLT).

When you obey the covenant that you vowed to keep in agreement with God's will for you, you must walk upright and righteous before God. This means being a devoted servant to God, delighted to do everything He directs you to do for Him because you love God with all your heart and soul!

God, You have my heart and soul. I love You so much!
I will do anything You ask of me. I am glad You are
my Father God and Lord over my life. I can't imagine
disappointing You in any way. I will therefore honor the
covenant between us.

DEVOTION 13

He alone is my rock and salvation, my defense and strong tower; I will not be shaken or disheartened (Psalm 62:2 AMP).

Do you have confidence and faith in God to be your strong tower of refuge and strength when the storms of life sweep over you? If you do, then you will immediately seek God's presence as your safe haven that will protect and shelter you until the heavy winds and rains the storms of life don't bother you any longer.

O my God, I was scared that the storms of life would drown me in the sea of despair, until I felt Your strong presence pull me out of the turbulent waters and save me. I am thankful that I can call on You, Lord, and be reassured that You are my dependable Rescuer. I receive such complete peace in my soul knowing You are my strong Tower of refuge!

DEVOTION 14

"With your unfailing love you lead the people you have redeemed. In your might, you guide them to your sacred home" (Exodus 15: 13 NLT).

The King of Glory is waiting at His castle gates to lead you by your righteous right hand to your new home, where you will live with the 'Great I Am' forever and ever. Everlasting peace awaits you as you worship with the angels before the throne of the Lord.

You will run through the heavenly gardens with a white robe, interwoven with gold wrapped around your glorified body. A crown of splendor will be on your head along with rings of silver on your toe, as your feet glide through the flowers that are clapping their hands, welcoming you in joyous delight.

I can't wait until You call me home to heaven, Lord, to be with You forever and ever! As I walk through the golden gates to the divine castle of the 'Great I Am', I imagine I will be singing and praising Your glorious Name above all names! I love You Lord so very much!

DEVOTIONAL 15

"I have told you all this so that you may have peace in
me. Here on earth you will have many trials and sorrows.
But take heart, because I have overcome the world"
(John 16:33 NLT).

Let the peaceful, calming presence of God wipe away all the
worries in your mind, like an eraser would do on a chalkboard. Never
again do you have to feel anxious and disturbed, if you make God the
most important part and start to your day!

What an awesome Friend I have in You, God! I can come
into Your gentle arms and be held in Your peaceful
presence, and feel all my worries and fears just melt
away, like an ice cube placed in hot water. I surrender
my life, Lord, to You. You can take better care of it than
I can!

DEVOTION 16

Looking for the blessed hope and glorious appearing for our great God and Savior Jesus Christ, who gave Himself up for us, so that He might redeem us from every lawless deed and purify for Himself His own special people, zealous for good works (Titus 2:13-14).

Jesus loves you so much that He gave up His perfect life in heaven to be born on earth a human baby destined to die at 33 years old to redeem you from eternal death in hell. You would have been cut off from the sunlight of Jesus' Spirit forever, but you have a wonderful Savior who gave up His life so you could live forever with Him.

Jesus, O Jesus, I am so in love with You, My Precious Savior and Redeemer of my life! I was headed to hell but You selflessly gave up Your life to save mine. I didn't deserve such an honor, Jesus. I was a nothing, a sinner who didn't care about You. I can only repay all the kindness, mercy, and grace You have shown me by giving up my life to be Your willing servant. Take me and use me to help others find You.

DEVOTIONAL 17

"So they were scattered because there was no shepherd;
and they became food for all the beasts of the field when
they were scattered. My shepherd wandered through all
the mountains, and on every high hill; yes, My flock was
scattered over the whole face of the earth, and no one
was seeking or searching for them" (Ezekiel 34:5-6).

The voice of the Lord is calling you to immediate action and the urgency is as if red lights and sirens are going off all around you. What is your delay in answering that call? Are you afraid of going out and being a shepherd to lead the Lord's sheep who have gone astray into the darkness of the enemy, the deceiver of mankind? They need a guiding light to help them find security in the presence of Jesus, and you are that guiding light! Why do you hesitate in serving God?

Holy Father God, I have been negligent in carrying
out Your orders to save Your sheep who are lost in
the darkness where the evil one has lead them astray.
Forgive me, Father, for I have sinned against You by
delaying my attempts at saving Your sheep. Help me
do Your will, Jesus. I am ready to go out and be Your
shepherd.

DEVOTIONAL 18

*Rejoice always and delight in your faith; be unceasing
and persistent in prayer; in every situation [no matter
the circumstances] be thankful and continually give
thanks; for this is the will of God for you in Christ Jesus*
(1 Thessalonians 5:16-18 AMP).

Have you ever written a love letter to God, thanking Him for
all the blessings He so lovingly gives you every day? If you haven't
written such a letter, what is keeping you from doing so? Don't delay
in writing it today. He needs to hear from you now! The Lord would
be so pleased to have you write to Him, telling Him all your feelings.

*Precious Father God, I will not delay any longer in
writing You a love letter, thanking You for all the
blessings You give me every day. I love You, God, so
much!*

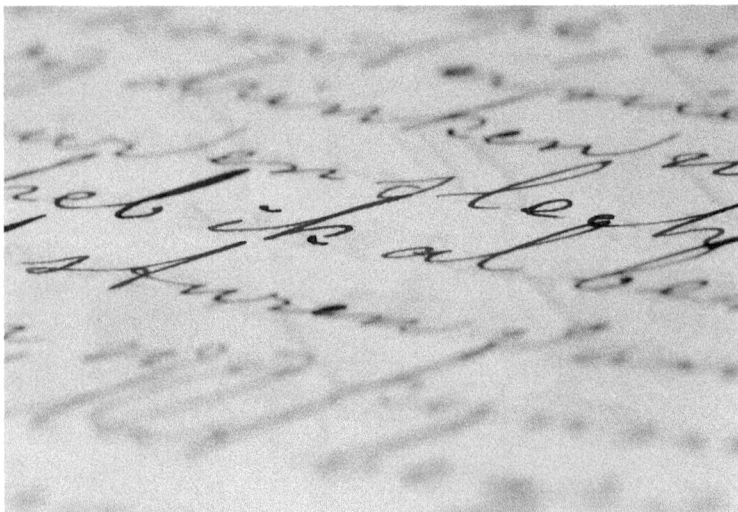

DEVOTIONAL 19

That my soul may sing praise to You and not be silent. O
Lord my God, I will give thanks to You forever
(Psalm 30:12 AMP).

God is good all the time, and all the time God is good! He never would think of allowing His children to fend for themselves against furious enemies who are attacking them. God will protect His children if they call on Him for help. He is faithful even when His children are not faithful to Him.

Don't be quiet in thanking God, and remember to be thankful when trials and tribulations come visiting you. God will not abandon you to fend for yourself when you are going through suffering in your life. He will hold you tenderly in His gentle arms of comfort, rubbing all the pain and distress away with His loving hands, until you feel serenity and peace in your heart and soul.

God, You give me strength when I am weak, hope when
I am in despair, courage when I am afraid, and peace
of mind instead of confusion. You are my awesome
Comforter, who never leaves me nor forsakes me in
times of trials and tribulations. I am thankful that I
have a God who is always faithful in providing for all my
needs. I love You!

DEVOTIONAL 20

"You are the God who sees me" (Genesis 16:13 NLT).

Those seven words above are packed with a tremendous amount of love. Hagar was running away from her mistress Sarai who had mistreated her when God met her at a spring in the desert. God comforted Hagar in her distress and informed her she was going to have a son who she was to name Ishmael.

Has God spoken to you when you were highly disturbed over something in your life, and just wanted to run away like Hagar did? Did He tell you to seek His comforting presence to heal your broken heart, where you will find the understanding and compassionate heart of a Father who loves you with an unfailing love? He will bind together all the broken pieces of your heart like super glue, and repair it better than it was before! Remember, God grieves right with you when you grieve.

Holy Father God, I love You so much! You take all the broken pieces of my heart, and fix them with Your healing hands of unfailing love. I have never had anyone who loves and cares about me like You do, Lord. Thank You for always being there for me. I couldn't make it through this uncertain life, where darkness waits around every corner to devour my soul, without You walking beside me holding my hand and keeping me safe.

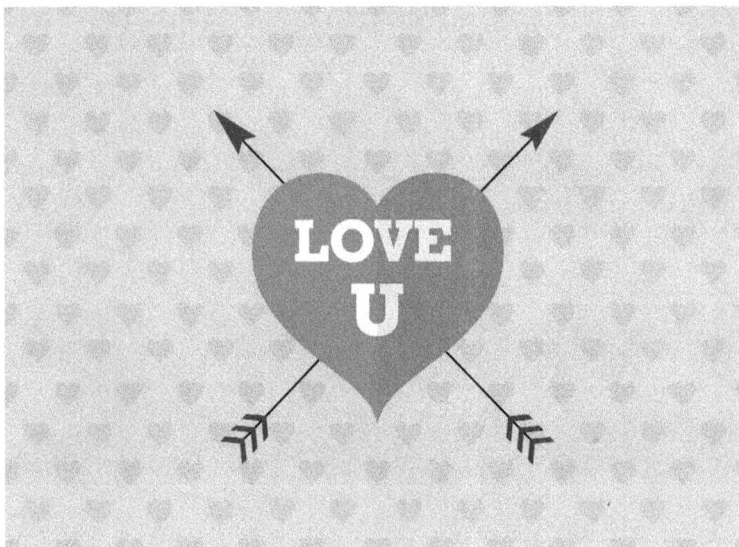

DEVOTIONAL 21

For nothing will be impossible with God (Luke 1:37 ESV).

Don't be afraid of any obstacle that blocks your attempts to achieve your goals in life. With God walking with you, the giant obstacles you are facing will be moved aside with one touch of God's mighty hand.

When you are climbing the mountains of life, remember to travel along with God, who is all the necessary equipment you need to be victorious as you climb up the mountains, and safely reach the top.

God, You are my great and powerful Overcomer of any
obstacles that block my way to achieving my goals in
life. But I need to remember to always take You with me,
Lord, so I can be victorious over anything that hinders
my progress or victories.

DEVOTIONAL 22

*But those who hope in the Lord will renew their
strength. They will soar on wings like eagles; they will
run and not grow weary, they will walk and not be faint*
(Isaiah 40:31).

When you feel about to faint from all the pressure of multiple
problems that weigh heavily on your mind, just imagine yourself soaring on the wings of an eagle with the Lord through fluffy white clouds
of peace and serenity.

As you trust in the Lord through faith, you will not allow difficulties in life to frustrate you anymore. You will feel joy and happiness
as you wait upon the Lord who will annihilate every obstacle that tries
to disrupt your peace of mind.

*Lord, You are my constant Companion! When I am
in trouble and need Your assistance to overcome any
problems that try to disturb my tranquility and peace,
I simply need to ask for help. My difficulties become a
distant memory with You in charge of them. I thank You
so much Lord for making all my days joyous and blessed.
I really, really, love You, Lord!*

DEVOTIONAL 23

"Behold, the virgin shall be with child, and bear a Son,
and they shall call His name Immanuel," which is
translated, "God with us" (Matthew 1:23).

What is important to you at Christmas? Is it decorating, making cookies or candy, buying presents for family and friends? Or is the birth of Jesus, the most important reason for you to celebrate Christmas? As a friend of mine always says, "Don't answer too quickly."

Faith without action is dead. You can go around and shout from the rooftops that you believe in Jesus Christ, but if that is all you are doing, then you are not really a disciple of Jesus. Jesus went around from town to town healing the sick and demon possessed. He spent time with the sinners, teaching them about God. He fed the people who followed Him. He died a prisoner's death on a cross so everyone's sins could be forgiven. He never abandoned anyone in need. He served and He calls you to a life of service as well.

Jesus, please help me to be more like You—concerned
about helping those in need. Sometimes I can be selfish
and self-centered. I am sorry for not helping more
people in Your precious Holy Name.

DEVOTIONAL 24

For our struggle is not against flesh and blood, but against the rulers, against the authorities, against the powers of this dark world against the spiritual forces of evil in the heavenly realms (Ephesians 6:12).

God can defeat the attacks of the evil one and his minions. God is your strong Rock of salvation when you are being tempted by the devil. But you must remember that the deceiver never does anything original under the sun. He has existed from the beginning of time, but has not learned his lesson yet. He keeps thinking in his twisted, depraved mind that he is more powerful than God. The reality of the opposite will never cease to be true. If you rebuke the devil in the Holy Name of Jesus, He will be forced to flee. Stand strong—God has your back!

Holy Father God, I am grateful You have my back. The devil and his helpers have to flee when I call on Your Name to help me. The devil knows You will kick his evil behind with one mighty kick of Your holy foot. Thank You for being my constant Companion and best friend. I love You, Jesus!

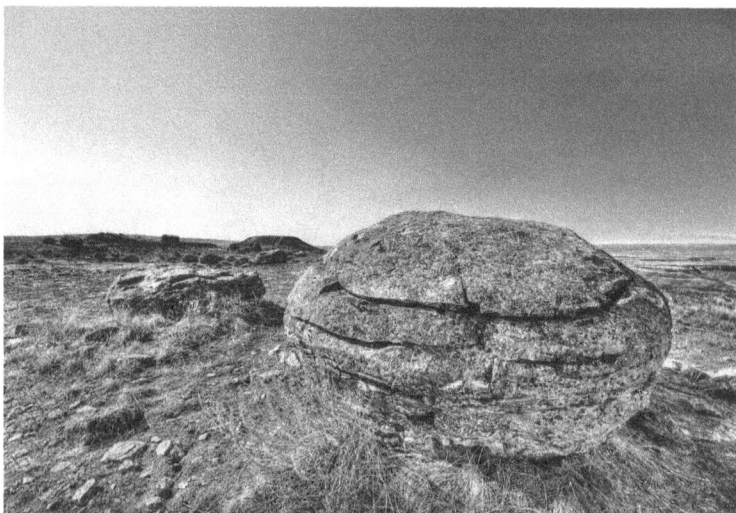

DEVOTIONAL 25

*For to us a child shall be born, to us a Son shall be given;
and the government shall be upon His shoulder, and His
name shall be called Wonderful Counselor, Mighty God,
Everlasting Father, Prince of Peace* (Isaiah 9:6 AMP).

It is amazing that Jesus would willingly surrender His life to die on a cross! Think about that for a moment. Do you find it astonishing that Jesus died for all sinners? Instead, He could have refused to give up His life for us, alternatively send His angels to wipe out every sinner on earth and doom us to hell for all eternity. (We deserved to die for our transgressions against God.) Only through the unfailing love of Jesus could mercy and grace be extended to us, to save us from our sins.

*Oh dear Jesus, I am so humbled and grateful to You for
saving a filthy wretch like me. I was one of the persons
who would have shouted loudly, "Crucify Him." I wasn't
remorseful one bit for my transgressions against God!
Only later when I was born again did I confess my sins to
You. I am so sorry Jesus that I treated You that way!*

DEVOTIONAL 26

Who shall separate us from the love of Christ? Shall
tribulations, or distress, or persecution, or famine, or
nakedness, or peril, or sword. As it is written: "For Your
sake we are killed all day long; we are accounted as sheep
for the slaughter." Yet in all these things we are more
than conquers through Him who loved us
(Romans 8:35-37).

God delighted to turn His Son Jesus over to death on a cross, where the blood from His wounds poured down upon your soul and wiped away all your filthy sins, cleansing your soul white as the newly-fallen snow.

What a priceless gift you were selflessly given by Jesus Christ that horrible day more than 2000 years ago. He was whipped, spat upon, a crown of thrones was placed upon His head, nails were driven into His hands and feet, and He was ridiculed by the Roman soldiers. But Jesus withstood it all to gain your freedom from your sins. You were given a love like no other!

Precious Heavenly Father, I am so sad that Jesus had to
suffer a horrendous death so my sins could be wiped
clean from the holy book of life forever. I know it was
predestined by You, but I still am sad my sins caused You
so much pain, Jesus! Thank You for the blessed life You
have given me.

DEVOTIONAL 27

*Christ is the visible image of the invisible God. He
existed before anything was created and is supreme over
all creation, for through him God created everything
in the heavenly realms and on earth. He made the
things we see and things we can't see—such as thrones,
kingdoms, rulers, and authorities in the unseen world.
Everything was created through him. . . . For God in all
his fullness was pleased to live in Christ, and through
him God reconciled everything to himself. He made
peace with everything in heaven and on earth by means
of Christ's blood on a cross*
(Colossians 1:15-16, 19-20 NLT).

Jesus Christ is the gift that keeps on giving at Christmas and
every day of your life. The more people you tell about Christ, the more
people they will tell, and pretty soon, there could be a world where
everyone could live in peace.

The choice is yours. Right now you have the choice to go out
and proclaim truth to those who never heard about the precious
name of Jesus. You don't know how much time you have left before
Jesus returns again. He could return today. Are you ready to receive
Him? Did you take care of His children?

*I hope I am pleasing in your eyes, Lord. Have I done
everything You asked me to do? I have tried to be a
faithful servant to You, Jesus. Please give me a willing
heart to reach more and more of Your children. I want
as many on earth as possible to be saved. I love You very
much, Jesus!*

DEVOTIONAL 28

You shall love the Lord your God with all your heart,
and with all your soul, and with all your strength
(Deuteronomy 6:5).

Hallelujah, hallelujah, the Lord, the mighty King of glory lives inside your soul. Nothing can penetrate you because your everlasting Father is the electrical fence that surrounds your soul, shocking anything that tries to harm you. When you belong to the Lord, you are His responsibility forever.

You are the Lord of lords, and King of kings! You are the
Name above all names, the great "I Am." You are alive
inside my soul, precious Father, through the Holy Spirit.
I never have to fear when You are guarding me. Nothing
can penetrate the protective fence You have around my
soul. Hallelujah, hallelujah, the mighty King of Glory is
with me forever!

DEVOTIONAL 29

*I will give thanks and praise to You, for I am fearfully
and wonderfully made; and my soul knows it very well.
My frame was not hidden from You, when I was being
formed in secret, and intricately and skillfully formed [as
if embroidered with many colors] in the depths of the
earth* (Psalm 139:14-15 AMP).

God's unfailing love formed you in the secret place where He
molded you with perfection and grace. You are His most precious and
beloved of all creations. (God doesn't make junk, only masterpieces.)
You are a beautiful, breathtaking woman whom God wanted to dis-
play for all the world to see as an expression of His outstanding art-
istry. You are a one-of-a-kind creation. There is no one like you in the
whole world!

*For so long, God, I didn't think I was worthy enough for
You to love me. I am thankful I have come to find out
You love me unconditionally, Father! I never want to be
away from Your loving presence, Lord!*

DEVOTIONAL 30

The Lord says, "I will rescue those who love me. I will
protect those who trust in my name. When they call on
me, I will answer; I will be with them in trouble. I will
reward them with a long life and give them my salvation"
(Psalm 91:14-16 NLT).

The Lord is your peaceful haven where you can stay and bask in His tranquil presence. You can rest in seclusion, feeling relaxed and undisturbed by your worries and troubles.

Take the initiative to seek the Lord and don't allow yourself to get bent out of shape like a contortionist who forces their body into weird shapes. Is it really worth it to try and handle anything alone? All you get for your self-dependence is agony. You were meant to be dependent on the Lord for everything.

Oh Lord, why do I allow myself to get stressed out over
problems in my life? You are always delighted to help
me Father, whenever I seek Your presence. I can be so
headstrong at times. Please direct my steps through this
uncertain life, Lord. I love You!

DEVOTIONAL 31

The way of the Lord is a stronghold to those with
integrity, but it destroys the wicked
(Proverbs 10:29 NLT).

Every day you have a choice to follow the ways of the Lord, which are as numerous as the stars that can safely guide you through the darkness of life. Or you can choose to follow the footsteps of the devil, which will lead you to a snare that will trap your soul in the decay of the abyss of hell forever. Who will you choose to follow today?

Sometimes, Lord, I lose sight of You along the pathways
of life, and stray away from You, and find myself headed
down a dark and scary path where the evil one waits for
me. When I ask You to help me, Lord, You come running
immediately to save me from the enemy. I am so glad I
belong to You, Father!

DEVOTIONAL 32

*As for God, His way is perfect; the word of the Lord is
proven; He is a shield to all those who trust in Him*
(2 Samuel 22:31 NKJV).

It is important to study the word of God to develop your soul.
If you don't seek a personal relationship with God, it will be like you
are walking to a special destination only to get lost on a dead-end road
forever. You are then wide open to spiritual deception from the devil.

*Dear heavenly Father, help me to always seek Your
glorious presence, where I can be refreshed daily by Your
spiritual food to recharge my soul. I need You, Lord! You
are a strong Shield that will protect me from the fiery
arrows of the devil that could pierce my soul with his
foul odor of corruption. I love You!*

DEVOTIONAL 33

"What do you mean, 'If I can'?" Jesus asked, "Anything is possible if a person believes" (Mark 9:23 NLT).

If you believe that anything is possible with God, then you will ask Him to meet your needs in the name of Jesus Christ. Maybe you want to go back to school or you need help financially. If so, then ask Him for help and once you ask, thank Him that it's already done. He will never turn you away and even if He says no to your requests, you will still enjoy your time with Him as you learn to listen and love Him even more.

Dear Jesus, I would have never believed my life could be so blessed. If I received everything I desired for my life, I would have sold myself short! You have helped me achieve all the goals I wanted, Jesus. Thank You, thank You, Lord, so very much for a wonderful life I live today in You.

DEVOTIONAL 34

You are of God, little children, and have overcome them, because He who is in you is greater than he who is in the world (1 John 4:4).

You are guilty by association if you have a relationship with Christ Jesus because the world will condemn you for believing in the Lord. You may someday be asked to reject Jesus, or else surrender your life. Are you ready to die for Jesus?

I hope and pray that someday, Jesus, if I am put to the test to reject You or die, that I would willingly die for You.